To my cat, Who Dey,
whom I was petting
when I first sharted.

It happened very
suddenly
and took you by surprise

The fart you thought
was coming out
was poop, in fart disguise

You tried to sneak
it out unheard by
leaning in your seat,

but when the moment
came to pass you felt
a troubling heat.

Your panicked mind begins to race. Your palms begin to sweat.

For just a moment you're unsure...

Oh no.
Your butt is wet.

Before you cry, or run and hide, before you fall apart.

Just take a moment to relax. Hey, everybody sharts!

I know a teacher who in class bent down to grab a book

I know a wealthy
CEO who tried to
hide a toot

while speaking to his board members, he sharted in his suit!

I know the singer of
a band who sang a
three-hour show.

He sharted while the sound was checked and didn't even know!

I've heard
the stories
far and wide,

sharts come
at any time.

An airport lounge,

a subway car,

Peruvian ziplines

so while you're feeling
all alone, this moment
is your chance.

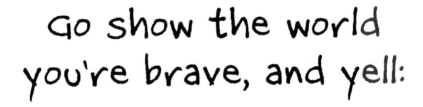

Go show the world
you're brave, and yell:

while some may gasp
and act appalled, you
know deep in their
hearts

They've all been there a time or two, because everybody sharts!

And suddenly you're not alone. No need to be ashamed!

For we all shart,
each one of us, and
so we are the same.

The End

Yay Hooray Productions, LLC was formed by a group of driven individuals convinced that they could change the world for the better with their collective ideas. A lawyer, a business owner, a web developer, and a nurse, all successful in their own fields, were inspired to pitch ideas on how to create something that people need. And then to create a successful business out of fulfilling that need. Unfortunately one of their members, John G, continually turned their attention away from serious, groundbreaking work with stories of various times he had pooped in his pants.

After enough wasted meeting time, the group collectively agreed that if John G promised never to mention sharting again, they'd publish his book. This is that book.

Soon after agreeing to complete this task, the other members were blown away by how much people around them talked about sharting. It was in the media, their favorite TV shows, even their children came home from school after sharting in their pants. John G proposed that this was not an accident. They just had been opened up to the truth; everybody sharts. It is the thing that binds us all together! What greater need is there in this world than the need for understanding and togetherness? Humility and self-love?

Now go show the world you're brave, take a photo with the following page, and post it to **#everybodysharts**

John G Ziplining in Peru.

I sharted here!

#everybodysharts

Printed in Great Britain
by Amazon

28498076R00018